PIANO SOLO

LITTLE WOMEN

MUSIC FROM THE MOTION PICTURE SOUNDTRACK

MUSIC BY
ALEXANDRE DESPLAT

Motion Picture Artwork © 2020 CTMG.
All Rights Reserved.

ISBN 978-1-5400-8988-5

Visit Hal Leonard Online at
www.halleonard.com

Contact us:
Hal Leonard
7777 West Bluemound Road
Milwaukee, WI 53213
Email: info@halleonard.com

In Europe, contact:
Hal Leonard Europe Limited
42 Wigmore Street
Marylebone, London, W1U 2RN
Email: info@halleonardeurope.com

In Australia, contact:
Hal Leonard Australia Pty. Ltd.
4 Lentara Court
Cheltenham, Victoria, 3192 Australia
Email: info@halleonard.com.au

CONTENTS

LITTLE WOMEN

By ALEXANDRE DESPLAT

PLUMFIELD

By ALEXANDRE DESPLAT

9

THE BEACH

By ALEXANDRE DESPLAT

CHRISTMAS MORNING

By ALEXANDRE DESPLAT

DANCE ON THE PORCH

By ALEXANDRE DESPLAT

THE BOOK

By ALEXANDRE DESPLAT

FATHER COMES HOME

By ALEXANDRE DESPLAT

Moderately slow

AMY

By ALEXANDRE DESPLAT

FRIEDRICH DANCES WITH JO

By ALEXANDRE DESPLAT

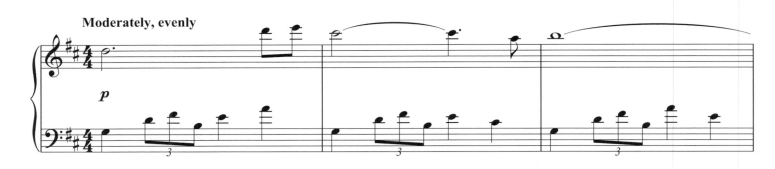

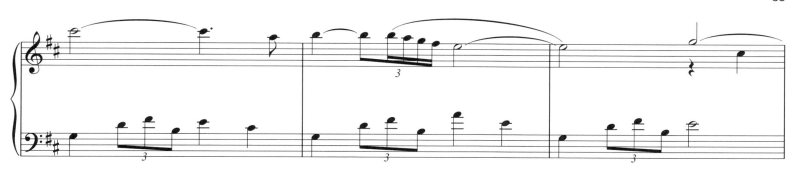

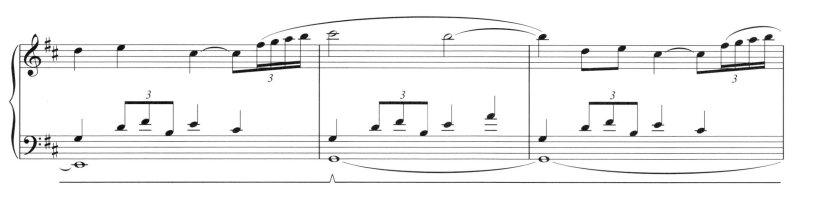

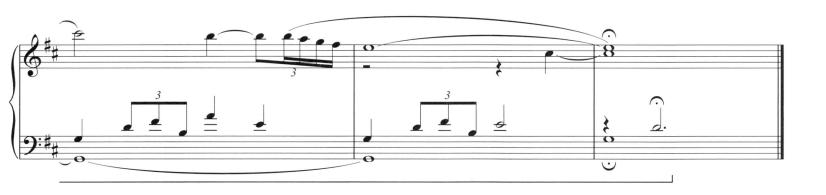

TELEGRAM

By ALEXANDRE DESPLAT

THEATRE IN THE ATTIC

By ALEXANDRE DESPLAT

LAURIE AND JO ON THE HILL

By ALEXANDRE DESPLAT

THE LETTER

By ALEXANDRE DESPLAT

Moderately slow, in 2

mp

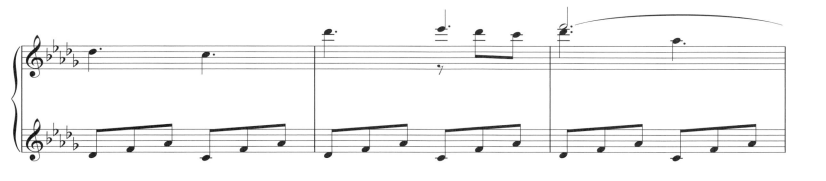

8va

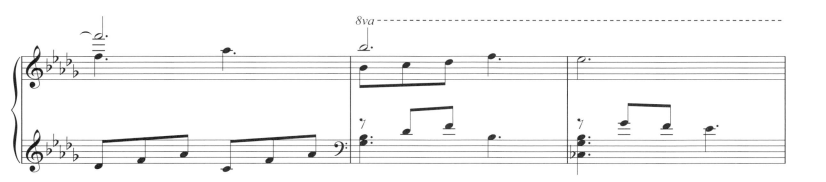

SNOW IN THE GARDEN

By ALEXANDRE DESPLAT

gradual cresc.

mf

JO WRITES

By ALEXANDRE DESPLAT

IT'S ROMANCE

By ALEXANDRE DESPLAT

DR. MARCH'S DAUGHTERS

By ALEXANDRE DESPLAT

WALTZ OP. 9, NO. 16

By FRANZ SCHUBERT

SONATA NO. 8 IN C MINOR, OP. 13

"Pathétique" Second Movement

By LUDWIG VAN BEETHOVEN

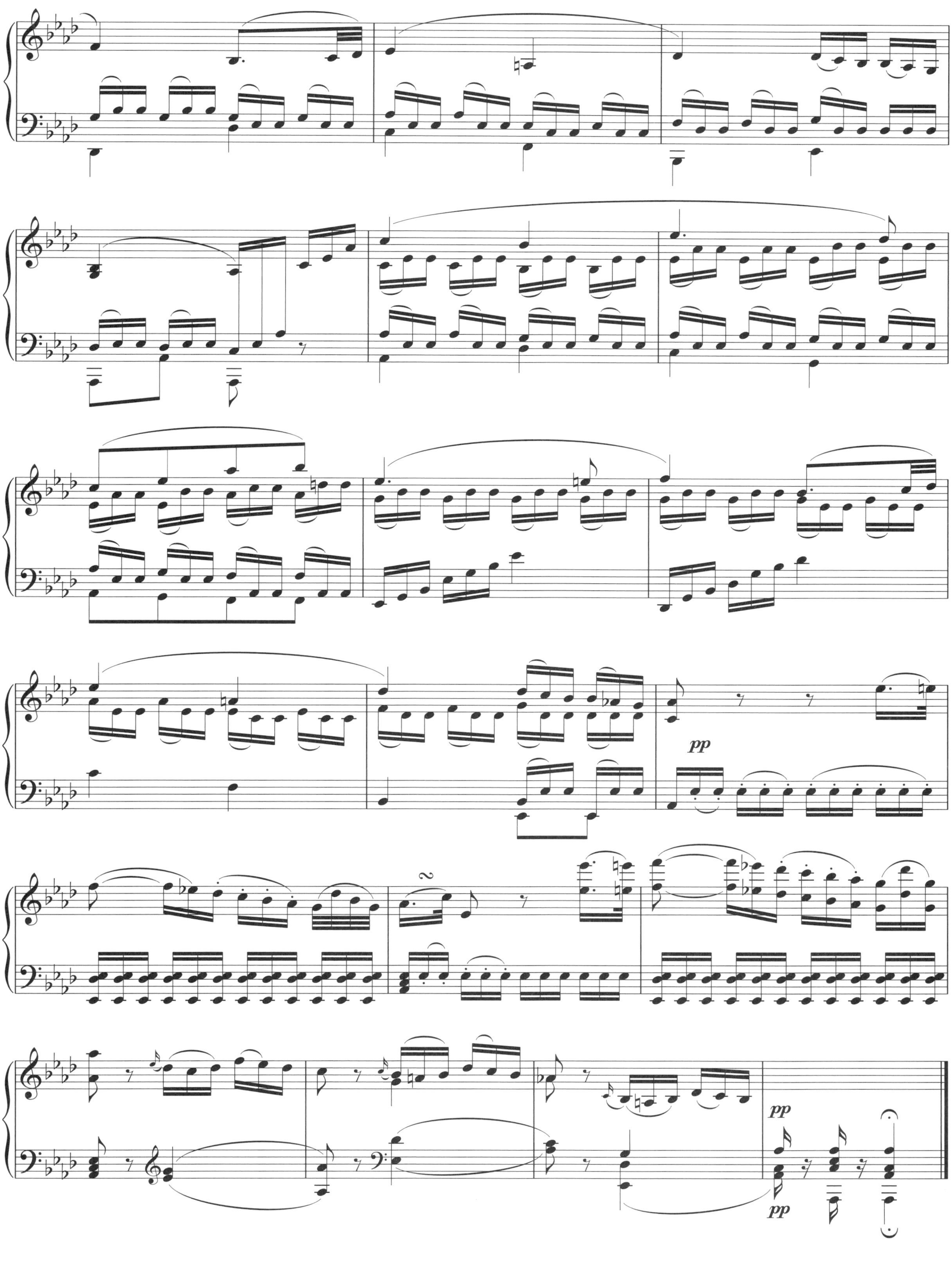
pp
pp
pp

WALTZ IN A-FLAT MAJOR
Op. 39, No. 15

By JOHANNES BRAHMS

NOCTURNE IN F-SHARP MAJOR
Op. 15, No. 2

By FREDERIC CHOPIN

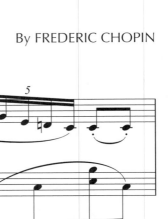

Larghetto

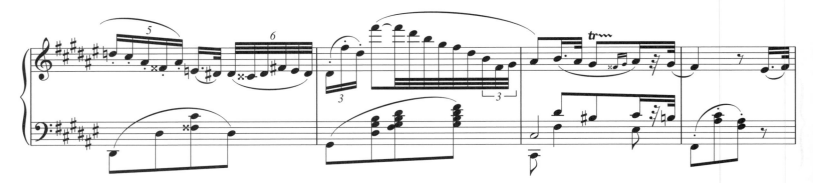

PAPILLONS OP. 2, NO. 10

By ROBERT SCHUMANN

VON FREMDEN LÄNDERN UND MENSCHEN

(From Foreign Lands and People)

from *Kinderszenen* Op. 15, No. 1

By ROBERT SCHUMANN